T H E   B O O K   O F

SMOOTHIES
JUICES & SHAKES

T H E   B O O K   O F

SMOOTHIES
JUICES & SHAKES

KATHRYN HAWKINS

HPBooks

HPBooks
A member of Penguin Group (USA) Inc.
375 Hudson Street, New York, New York 10014, USA
Penguin Group (Canada), 10 Alcorn Avenue, Toronto,
Ontario M4V 3B2, Canada (a division of Pearson Penguin
Canada Inc.)
Penguin Books Ltd., 80 Strand, London WC2R 0RL, England
Penguin Group Ireland, 25 St. Stephen's Green, Dublin 2,
Ireland (a division of Penguin Books Ltd.)
Penguin Group (Australia), 250 Camberwell Road,
Camberwell, Victoria 3124, Australia (a division of Pearson
Australia Group Pty. Ltd.)
Penguin Books India Pvt. Ltd., 11 Community Centre,
Panchsheel Park, New Delhi—110 017, India
Penguin Group (NZ), cnr. Airborne and Rosedale Roads,
Albany, Auckland 1310, New Zealand (a division of Pearson
New Zealand Ltd.)
Penguin Books (South Africa) (Pty.) Ltd., 24 Sturdee Avenue,
Rosebank, Johannesburg 2196, South Africa
Penguin Books Ltd., Registered Offices: 80 Strand, London
WC2R 0RL, England

An imprint of **Chrysalis** Books Group plc

Photographer: Philip Wilkins
Home Economist and Stylist: Mandy Phipps
Editor: Katherine Edelston
Designer: Cara Hamilton
Production: Don Campaniello
Filmset and reproduction by: Anorax Imaging Ltd

ISBN: 1-55788-459-5

PRINTING HISTORY
HPBooks trade paperback edition / April 2005

Notice: The information contained in this book is true and
complete to the best of our knowledge. All recommendations
are made without any guarantees on the part of the author or
the publisher. The author and publisher disclaim all liability in
connection with the use of this information.

Printed and bound in China

10 9 8 7 6 5 4 3 2 1

CONTENTS

INTRODUCTION

With more and more emphasis on the benefit of increasing our intake of fruit and vegetables, and our need to maximize our liquid intake, we must think of new ways to include them in our diet. Smoothies, juices, and shakes are a great way to do this. The term "smoothie" refers to drinks made in a blender, and they can be made of fruit juice and pulp; sweet or savory; with added dairy and non-dairy ingredients; extra healthful and nutritious, or just a little bit naughtier. Most can be drunk at any time of the day, others make a great meal-in-a-glass, and some can be so thick you might need to use a spoon! So, if you are in need of inspiration and lacking enthusiasm, then take a look at this delicious selection of drinks, there's one to suit just about every requirement; they are guaranteed to put you on track and feeling great. All you need to get started is a blender, and if you really get into it, then it's worth investing in a juice extractor, so you can enjoy the maximum nutritional benefits.

NUTRITION

We all need to drink in order to stay alive and in good working order, but many of us are unaware of exactly what we're consuming when we reach for a ready-made drink off the shelf. Many drinks we consume whether in a can, bottle, or carton, or powdered drinks from a jar or package, even tea or coffee, are full of "added" ingredients often unnecessary and detrimental to our health. Sugar is the first ingredient to look at, be it in the refined form of sucrose or artificial form as sweeteners, too much sugar in the diet is a major cause of tooth decay and can lead to obesity and all the associated health risks. Although sugar provides us with energy, it is 100 percent pure carbohydrate and nothing else—there are no other nutritional benefits—a healthy diet should provide all the energy we need

Below: Citrus and other fruit is a healthy and natural source of unprocessed sugar, known as fructose.

without eating sugar. Fruit and vegetables contain natural sugar called fructose in varying amounts, and it is far better for your health to rely on this form of sugar for your energy. If you do find it necessary to add a little more sweetness then choose honey or maple syrup which do have trace elements, but you will soon get used to the natural sweetness of ingredients and you will appreciate the fresher flavors. A word of warning, drinking too much fruit juice can give your system an overload of fructose, so if you suffer from sugar intolerance (hypoglycemia), diabetes, or Candidiasis, you should be wary of the amount you consume and you should check recommended intakes with your physician.

Although a small amount of fat in the diet is essential for good health—vitamins A and D are fat soluble, and minerals like calcium are richly supplied in dairy produce—too much fat will lead to weight gain and increased risk of heart disease. The fats found in many milk shakes and yogurt drinks are usually from animal or dairy sources, and thus contain saturated fat and cholesterol. Keep the intake of these fats to a minimum and try using

Below: Most fruits, including berries, are a rich source of the vitamins our bodies require to stay fit and healthy.

more nondairy products in the diet instead. Caffeine is a naturally occurring substance found in coffee, cocoa, tea, maté, and the cola bean. It is a diuretic—causing dehydration and nutrient depletion—and acts as a stimulant—giving a "lift" and lessens tiredness, also stimulating the central nervous system, kidneys, and heart. It can also be addictive, and withdrawal symptoms such as headache and irritability are not uncommon when giving up the intake altogether.

There has been lots of discussion regarding the use of artificial additives in the manufacture of foodstuffs, and the effect they have on the body. Food colorings have been long associated with hyperactivity in children, and side effects for those sensitive to additives range from eczema and asthma to headaches, gastric disorders, and general malaise. Even if you don't have any obvious symptoms, it is worth thinking about what you're putting into your body and asking yourself how you feel about ingesting unnatural substances, and also reconsider the potential hidden damages that might occur in the future.

Don't forget fiber in your diet as it is important for good digestion. Blended fruit and vegetable retains all the fiber held within but if it is peeled then this extra fiber intake is

lost, as it is when juiced. Most fruit contains more fiber than vegetables and is easier to digest, so fruit smoothies are an excellent fiber source. You can add extra fiber to smoothies—see Optional Extras (page 11)—but if your diet contains other sources of fiber from beans and whole grains, then you don't have to do this every time.

With all this in mind, smoothies can make good nutritional sense mainly because if you're making one then you know exactly what is in it. Smoothies are delicious and packed full of the natural, unprocessed nutrients that promote a healthy diet. Quick and easy to prepare, most recipes simply require fresh ingredients available from any local grocery

store. You will probably find that smoothies are one of the easiest ways to create a more nutritiously balanced diet without you even realizing it. Vitamin pills may have their place, but fruit and vegetables provide a better means of taking on board all the nutrients our bodies need day to day, and the trace elements that are so vital to our health.

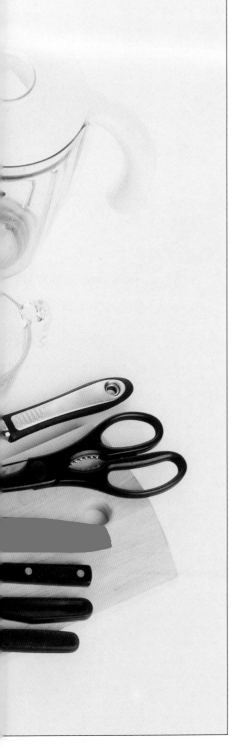

EQUIPMENT

Making your own smoothies can easily become part of your daily routine, and you don't need much equipment, so even the smallest of kitchens can accommodate what you will need.

A blender is designed to liquidize or "pulp" what ever is put into them by "shredding" at a high speed. You will find free standing blenders with a large removable pitcher made from glass or sturdy plastic with a metal or plastic blade, set on a motor with variable speeds—more expensive models have a blade, which is strong enough to crush ice. (NOTE: never assume that your blender can crush ice, always check the manufacturer's information, otherwise you may seriously damage the motor.) Some food processors and mixers have a blender attachment, which fits along side or on top of the main processing bowl. There are also smaller hand held blenders, which either come with a small canister or bowl to fit on to while blending, or which are free standing enabling you to blend in your own pitcher or container.

If you don't have a blender or food processor, then you can simply mash ripe fruit, like bananas, mango, or avocado, with a fork and then mix them with other ingredients. The resulting smoothie will be thicker and have more texture. You can also strain certain types of fruit, like berries and currants, through a fine-mesh strainer or even through clean cheesecloth.

JUICE EXTRACTORS

To juice or not to juice? That is the question: the closer you stay to the freshest ingredients the more nutritional benefits you will reap, and this is worth bearing in mind when it comes to fruit and vegetable juices. As soon as you start preparing fruit or vegetables, by simply cutting or peeling, various nutrients start being lost as they are easily destroyed by air and light. Not all fruit and vegetables are suitable for blending, for example, harder textured foods like apples and

Left: *Making your own smoothies and juices requires little specialist equipment and is quick and easy to do.*

carrots will pulverize but not soften completely as they are more fibrous. So if you want to have a wider choice with maximum nutritional benefit then perhaps you should think about making your own juices, and there are several different types of machine for juice extraction:

Centrifugal—reasonably priced, electrically powered, high-speed juicer that shreds up fruit and vegetables, and then spins the pulp at high speed in a meshed basket, separating out the juice into a pitcher, while the pulp stays in the basket. They need thorough cleaning to prevent them becoming clogged. The resulting juice is quite thick and creamy, and the pulp remains wet.

Masticating—more expensive but more efficient, high-speed manual or electric juicer, which finely chops into a paste and then squeezes the juice through a mesh at the bottom. This type copes well with skin, peel, and seeds.

Hydraulic Press—expensive, manual or electric, very efficient high-speed juicer that finely chops and then presses out the juice under great pressure, resulting in a high-quality filtered juice and dry pulp.

Slow-turning or wheatgrass juicer—operates in a very different manner than high-speed juicers. A motor slowly turns a blade inside the juicer, which presses juices from leafy greens, sprouts, wheatgrass, and soft vegeta-

Above: Fresh fruits, such as melon, kiwi, and papaya, are both delicious and a great source of fiber.

bles, rather than masticating them, and the resulting juice is less oxidized than if it had been produced from a high-speed juicer.

Citrus Juicer—extracts juice from all citrus fruit. They can be electric—halved fruit is held on a rotating cone causing the juice to fall into a container below—or manual. The resulting juice is clearer and thinner than juice made in other types of juicer.

Always keep your drink-making equipment clean and dry to avoid contamination. If you have been using strongly flavored ingredients, make sure you wash out the container thoroughly so that these flavors don't taint future drinks. Some juice, such as carrot or beet, may cause discoloration. Some of this can be removed by rubbing with a cloth dipped in vegetable oil, and passing chopped apple through equipment acts as a cleanser, helping to remove odors and color staining. However, if time is short, then there are a wide selection of ready-prepared organic and nonorganic juices on the market. But don't forget that even 100 percent juice has been processed to a point that most of the vitamins and minerals listed on the label are additives, and they do work out more expensive than buying the raw ingredients.

CHOOSING, PREPARATION, AND STORAGE

Choose the best quality ingredients you can afford. Avoid damaged, bruised, or wilting produce, and items past their "sell-by" date. Buying large quantities may also turn out to be a false economy—it is better to buy little and often for maximum freshness. Smoothies and juices are best prepared and drunk as soon as possible, and so it is better nutritionally to make only the amount necessary to suit your immediate needs. If you do need to store the drink, keep it for a few hours only, well sealed, in the refrigerator, and add a few drops of lemon juice to fruit and vegetable mixes to aid preservation. Look out for ripe, mature produce that will be easier to digest and contains the most nutrients. Digestion can be improved further by drinking fresh fruit and vegetable smoothies on an empty stomach—30 minutes before or after a meal, or as a between-meals snack.

Try and use organic ingredients where possible as in a lot of cases the skin and seeds of the fruit and vegetable are used to obtain maximum nutrition. Although "organics" tend to be more expensive, their advantage is that they have been exposed to only limited chemical treatments or waxes during growth and trans-

Below: Blended drinks can be both sweet and savory. When using vegetables always try to pick organic varieties.

portation, and it means that you can safely ingest whole produce without fear of taking in a dose of chemicals. If you can't buy organic produce, then make sure you wash and scrub the skins well, or peel completely. Thicker-skinned produce is not as easily affected because the chemicals can't penetrate the inner flesh as readily, and the skin is usually discarded anyway. For convenience, you can also use frozen fruit, thawed, or while still frozen—if you do thaw the fruit remember to save the juice as well. Canned fruit in natural juice is also a good standby, and naturally dried fruit can be soaked and blended to add sweetness and extra fiber— avoid dried fruit preserved with sulfur dioxide; although this looks brighter and more appealing, the preservative has a detrimental effect on the absorption of B vitamins in the body.

OPTIONAL EXTRAS

There are a whole load of additional ingredients you can add to your smoothies to change texture, add and enhance flavor, increase nutrition, or simply cool it down.

"Watering down"—smoothies can be a bit on the thick side for some palates so, depending on the recipe, you might want to thin the texture down a bit. Still mineral water works best for straight fruit and vegetable mixtures, whereas adding a little more dairy or nondairy milk to other

smoothies is an obvious liquidizer. Add sparkle with fizzy mineral water or low-calorie lemonade, and tonic water is a good choice for cocktail mixtures. Cold herb and fruit teas will not only act as "thinners" but can add extra flavor at the same time.

Cooling Down—when the heat is on or to pack a punch at your party, pouring the smoothie over ice cubes or crushed ice in a glass will have an immediate effect. If your blender is strong enough, you can blend ice cubes at the same time as your other ingredients to make a "slushy" iced smoothie, or freeze small pieces of fresh fruit or small quantities of juice in ice cube trays, and add these to the blender for an even juicier result.

Extra Flavor—fresh herbs, ginger, and freshly ground spices blended with your other smoothie ingredients can set your taste buds tingling. Add a little sea salt and freshly ground black pepper, if necessary, to savory combinations to bring out natural flavors, and a small amount of maple syrup or honey can take the edge off any sharp fruitiness.

Extra Nutrition—there are many other ingredients you can add to improve the vitality of your drink and meet your specific nutritional requirements; here are a few you might like to consider:
• Acidophilus—a probiotic, which unlike antibiotics is a beneficial bacteria that promotes good health. It is best taken after a bacterial infection or after a course of antibiotics and is particularly beneficial if suffering from digestive problems. Available from most drug and health food stores in capsule form, which usually requires storing in the refrigerator. It is now included in several ready-made drinks and yogurt products, but these often contain sugar which can have a detrimental effect.
• Bee pollen—a natural antibiotic and good general tonic. It is highly nutritious and revitalizing containing plenty of protein and essential amino acids. It is available as loose powder, granules, or tablet form, and can be easily incorporated in drinks. NOTE: it can cause an allergic reaction to pollen-sensitive individuals.
• Brewers' yeast—a byproduct of beer brewing. Exceptionally rich in B vitamins, with high levels of iron, zinc, magnesium, and potassium. Available in pill form or powder. Highly concentrated and an excellent pick-me-up. The flavor is strong so it needs to be mixed carefully with other ingredients to temper it down. NOTE: it is high in purines so should be avoided by gout sufferers.
• Echinacea—a native plant of North America and has been recommended by herbalists for many years to support a healthy immune system. A great all-rounder with antiviral and antibacterial properties. Comes in capsules and in extracts taken in drops, so it is easy to add to drinks. NOTE: echinacea is not recommended for use during pregnancy or when breastfeeding.
• Eggs—can be added to give extra protein and substance. Always use the freshest eggs and choose free-range or organic varieties. Remember eggs contain cholesterol so if you are on a restricted diet then they should be avoided. NOTE: raw egg should not be eaten by the elderly, children, babies, pregnant women, or those with an impaired immune system as there can be a risk of contracting salmonella.
• Ginseng—a herbal product taken from the roots of the plant grown in Russia, Korea, and China. The active constituents are ginsenosides, which are reputed to stimulate the hormones responsible for empowering the system and increasing the capacity for work. Ginseng is available in dry root form for grinding or ready powdered. NOTE: it should not be taken by those suffering from hypertension.
• Nuts—these are the dried fruit of various trees and so are richly packed with nutrients and nourishment. They are one of the most concentrated forms of protein available and are rich in vitamin B1, B6, and E, and many minerals. They do have a high-fat content, mostly polyunsaturated, however coconut, Brazil, cashew, peanut, and macadamia nuts do contain more saturated fat, so should be used sparingly. Almonds are particularly easy to digest. Finely chop or grind the nuts just before using for maximum freshness, and store in the refrigerator to prevent them going rancid.

• Seeds—high in flavor, texture, and nutritional content, containing a good supply of essential fatty acids (EFAs). Best purchased in small amounts as their fat content makes them go rancid quickly; keep airtight and in the refrigerator. Prepare them just before use for maximum benefit. Pumpkin (pepitas), sesame, and sunflower seeds work especially well in smoothies. Flaxseed is particularly beneficial as it has one of the richest sources of Omega-3 EFAs—57 percent more than oily fish. You can buy the seeds from health food stores and these can be ground just before using, or the oil—this has to be stored in the refrigerator—can easily be stirred into a smoothie.

• Sprouts—simply the seed of a variety of plants ranging from the sunflower to the mung bean, which have been fed a little water, given a little warmth, and have started to grow. By eating these sprouts you are able to tap into all the energy the young shoots have and give yourself a boost of vitality. Sprouts are full of vitamins, minerals, proteins, and carbohydrates. You can easily sprout your own seeds, but you'll find bags of ready-sprouted at health food stores. Sprouts are fairly soft so they will blend easily in savory smoothies for added zip.

• Oats—sold in the form of whole grain, rolled, flaked, ground, or oatmeal. They are an exceptionally rich grain—high in protein, vitamin B complex, vitamin E, potassium, calcium, phosphorus, iron, and zinc. Easy to digest and able to soothe the digestive tract. Toasted oatmeal has a nutty flavor and is ideal for smoothies. NOTE: oats should be avoided by those on a gluten-free diet.

• Wheat bran and germ—wheat bran is the outside of the wheat grain removed during milling. It is very high in fiber and adds bulk to the diet. It is bland in taste but adds a crunchy texture to whatever it is added to. Wheat germ, from the center of the grain, is very nutritious and easy to digest. It has a mild flavor and is excellent added to smoothies to boost nutrition. Highly perishable, it needs to be stored in the refrigerator once opened. NOTE: keep intake of bran to moderate levels as it can prevent certain nutrients from being absorbed if consumed in large doses.

Below: Savory ingredients, such as nuts, are a great source of protein and create filling and healthful drinks.

MERRY BERRY

generous ³/₄ cup strawberries
³/₈ cup raspberries, thawed if frozen, juices reserved
³/₈ cup blackberries, thawed if frozen, juices reserved
³/₈ cup blueberries, thawed if frozen, juices reserved
few ice cubes, to serve

Hull the strawberries, raspberries, and black-berries, if necessary. Wash the fruits and pat dry with paper towels, if using fresh.

Reserve a few fruits for decoration and place all the remaining fruit in a blender. If the fruit has been frozen, add the juices as well.

Blend for a few seconds until smooth. Pour over ice into a large serving glass. If desired, thread the reserved fruit on a small skewer or toothpick and serve with the juice.

Serves 1

LOVE APPLE CRUSH

1 ⅛ cups strawberries
⅔ cup freshly pressed apple juice or the yield from
  2 eating apples, juiced
strawberry leaves, to decorate (optional)

Wash the strawberries and pat dry with paper towels (reserving 1 or 2 for decoration); remove the hulls. Place on a tray and freeze for 40 minutes, until firm.

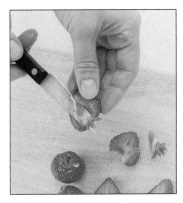

When ready to serve, place the frozen strawberries in a blender (reserving 1 or 2 for decoration).

Pour in the apple juice. Blend until smooth and slushy. Pile into a serving glass and decorate with reserved strawberries and leaves, if liked.

Serves 1

BERRY ORANGE

2 medium oranges
1/2 cup cranberries, thawed if frozen, juices reserved
3/8 cup raspberries, thawed if frozen, juices reserved
1 teaspoon honey (optional)

Peel the orange, removing as much of the white pith as possible. Chop coarsely, discarding any seeds, and reserve in a pitcher with the juices until needed.

Wash and pat dry the cranberries and raspberries if fresh, and remove stems and hulls, if necessary. Place in a blender and if the fruit has been frozen, add the juices.

Add the orange and blend until smooth. Taste and sweeten with the honey if necessary. Pour into 2 glasses to serve.

Serves 2

TIP: this is a fairly thick smoothie, so you may prefer to water it down with either some still mineral water or freshly pressed orange juice.

TASTE OF THE TROPICS

¹/₂ medium pineapple
1 small or "mini" mango
1 kiwifruit

Peel and core the pineapple and chop the flesh coarsely. Slice the flesh off the smooth flat central seed of the mango, then peel and chop.

Peel the skin from the kiwifruit and cut into 4 pieces. (Reserve 2 slices for garnish).

Place the remaining kiwifruit in a blender, along with the mango and pineapple. Blend until smooth and thick, then pile into 2 glasses. Thread the reserved kiwifruit onto toothpicks to garnish (if liked) and serve with a spoon.

Serves 2

VARIATION: if you prefer a thinner smoothie, water this recipe down with a little still mineral water.

PASSIONATE PAPAYA

¹/₂ medium papaya
¹/₂ lime
1 Golden passion fruit

Peel the papaya and scoop out the black seeds. Reserve 1 or 2 slices, then coarsely chop the remaining flesh, and place in a blender.

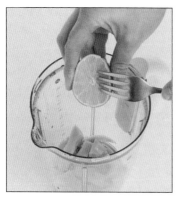

Remove a thin slice from the lime and set aside. Juice the lime and pour over the papaya.

Halve the passion fruit and scoop the seeds into the blender. Blend until smooth and then serve decorated with the reserved lime and papaya.

Serves 1

QUEEN PEACH

1 ripe peach
$\frac{1}{2}$ Queen (baby) pineapple or 4 slices from a
  medium fruit
1 apple banana or small ripe banana

Wash and pat dry the peach, and cut in half. Remove the pit and coarsely chop the flesh, reserving 1 or 2 small slices for decoration, if desired.

Peel the pineapple and chop coarsely. Peel the banana and chop coarsely.

Place all the fruit in a blender and blend until thick, creamy, and smooth. Pour into a large glass, decorate with the reserved peach slices, and serve with a spoon.

Serves 1

COOL GREEN MELON MIX

1/2 green melon such as Galia
1/4 honeydew melon
2/3 cup freshly pressed apple juice or the yield from
   2 eating apples, juiced
8 medium fresh mint leaves, plus a small sprig for
   garnish (optional)
few ice cubes, to serve
1 strawberry, for garnish (optional)

Scoop out the seeds from the melon.

Cut into slices, remove the skin, and chop the flesh coarsely. Place in a blender.

Pour in the apple juice. Wash and pat dry the mint leaves and add to the blender. Blend for a few seconds until smooth. Pour over ice and decorate with a sprig of mint and a strawberry (if liked). Serve with a straw.

Serves 2

—— SWEET MELON ITALIANO ——

¹/₂ orange melon such as cantaloupe or Charantais
2 medium oranges
6 large fresh basil leaves, plus extra for garnish
few ice cubes, to serve

Scoop out the seeds from the melon. Cut into slices, remove the skin, and chop coarsely. Place in a blender.

Peel the oranges, removing as much of the white pith as possible. Chop coarsely, discarding any seeds, and add to the blender.

Wash and pat dry the basil and add to the blender. Blend for a few seconds, until smooth, and pour into a large glass over ice. Serve decorated with basil, if liked.

Serves 1

── GINGERY WATERMELON ──

2-inch thick slice watermelon
4 oz red seedless grapes
1/2-inch piece fresh ginger
few ice cubes, to serve

Peel the watermelon and chop coarsely. Remove the seeds and discard. Place the flesh in a blender.

Wash and pat dry the grapes and add to the blender.

Peel and grate the ginger into the blender and blend for a few seconds, until smooth. Pour over ice in a large glass to serve.

Serves 1

VARIATION: red grapes are very sweet but, if preferred, seedless green or black grapes can be used.

BLUE ORANGE

1¹/₈ cups blueberries, thawed if frozen, juice reserved
  (plus extra for garnish)
2 medium oranges
1 teaspoon maple syrup (optional)
few ice cubes, to serve

If using fresh blueberries, wash, pat dry, and place in a blender. If the fruit has been frozen, add the juices as well.

Reserve a small slice of orange for decoration and then peel the oranges, slicing off as much of the white pith as possible. Chop coarsely, discarding any seeds, and place in the blender.

Blend for a few seconds, until smooth. Taste and add maple syrup, if using. Pour over ice in a large glass to serve. Thread the reserved orange slice and a few blueberries onto a toothpick and use to garnish (if liked).

Serves 1

ALMOND CHERRY FRAPPE

1½ cups fresh sweet cherries
⅔ cup freshly pressed apple juice or the yield from
  2 eating apples, juiced
few drops pure almond extract

Wash and pat dry the cherries, and remove the pits.

Place on a tray and freeze for about 30 minutes, until firm.

Transfer the frozen cherries to a blender, pour in the apple juice, and add a few drops almond extract. Blend until smooth and then pile into a serving glass.

Serves 1

TOMATO SALAD

8 ripe medium tomatoes on the vine
2 celery stalks
2 sprigs fresh parsley
6 whole fresh chives
dash of balsamic vinegar (optional)

Wash and pat dry the tomatoes. Remove the stems and chop coarsely. Place in a blender.

Wash and dry the celery; trim and slice, and add to the tomatoes.

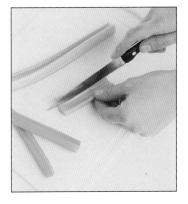

Rinse the herbs and pat dry. Using scissors, chop the herbs into the blender and blend until smooth. Add balsamic vinegar if using, mix well, and pour into serving glasses.

Serves 2

- FRUITY CARROT WITH GINGER -

2 medium oranges
1/2-inch piece fresh ginger
2/3 cup freshly pressed apple juice or the yield from
  2 eating apples, juiced
2/3 cup freshly pressed carrot juice or the yield from
  2 medium carrots

Peel and segment the oranges, removing as much of the white pith as possible. Chop coarsely, discarding any seeds, and place in a blender.

Peel and coarsely chop the ginger, and then add to the blender.

Pour in the apple and carrot juices and blend until smooth. Pour into 1 or 2 glasses and serve.

Serves 1-2

— WHEATGRASS & PINEAPPLE —

¹/₄ ripe medium pineapple
4 fresh mint leaves
2-inch round wheatgrass (see page 32)
still mineral water, well chilled, to taste

Peel and core the pineapple. Chop the flesh
coarsely and place in a blender.

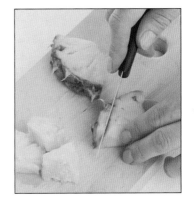

Wash and pat dry the mint leaves and place
in the blender. Set aside while preparing the
wheatgrass.

Wash and pat dry the wheatgrass and then
juice in a slow turning juicer. Add the juice
to the pineapple and mint. Blend until thick
and smooth. Serve at once, topped off with
mineral water, if preferred.

Serves 1

DEEP PURPLE

7 oz cooked peeled baby beet in natural juice
²/₃ cup freshly pressed apple juice or the yield from
  2 eating apples, juiced
1 teaspoon fennel seeds
few ice cubes, to serve

Coarsely chop the beet.

Place in a blender with the juices from the package. Pour in the apple juice.

Crush the fennel seeds and add to the blender. Blend for a few seconds until smooth, and pour over ice in serving glasses.

Serves 2

TIP: beet is a rich and powerful cleanser so serve in small measures. You can make your own beet juice for this recipe using 4 oz fresh beet—this will make a very concentrated juice drink. Make sure you use cooked beet in natural juice and avoid those pickled in vinegar.

GUACAMOLE IN A GLASS

1/2 lime
1 scallion
6 oz ripe cherry tomatoes on the vine
6 sprigs fresh cilantro
dash of Tabasco sauce
1 small ripe avocado

Extract the juice from the lime and set aside. Wash and pat dry the scallion and tomatoes. Trim the scallion and chop the white and green parts coarsely. Place in a blender.

Remove the stems from the tomatoes, quarter, and place in the blender. Wash and pat dry the cilantro and add to the blender along with a dash of Tabasco sauce.

Halve the avocado, remove the pit and peel; chop coarsely and place in the blender with the lime juice. Blend until thick, creamy, and smooth. Transfer to a large glass and serve with a spoon.

Serves 1

TIP: remember that avocados discolor quickly so prepare all the other ingredients before cutting the avocado.

AVOCADO PEAR

1 small lemon
1 ripe sweet pear
1 small ripe avocado
2/3 cup freshly pressed apple juice or the yield from
  2 eating apples, juiced

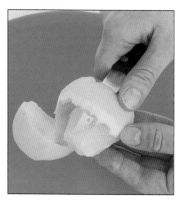

Peel the lemon, removing as much of the white pith as possible. Chop the flesh and remove any seeds. Place in a blender.

Working quickly, peel, core, and chop the pear and add to the lemon.

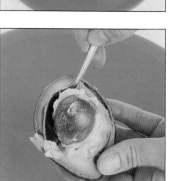

Halve the avocado, remove the pit and peel; chop coarsely and place in the blender with the lime and apple juices. Blend until smooth and serve in a large glass.

Serves 1

TIP: if the avocado is not very ripe you may have difficulty removing the pit, so sharply strike the pit with the blade of a knife and twist the knife to remove the pit.

RED FENNEL COOLER

8 medium ripe tomatoes on the vine
3 celery stalks with leaves
²/₃ cup cold fennel herb tea
few ice cubes, to serve

Wash and pat dry the tomatoes. Remove the stems and chop coarsely. Place in a blender.

Wash and dry the celery, reserving the leaves, then trim and slice the remainder and add to the blender.

Pour in the cold tea and blend for a few seconds until smooth. Pour over ice to serve, with reserved celery leaves to garnish.

Serves 2

TIP: herb teas make excellent ingredients for "watering down" and they also add flavor. For a more concentrated drink, make your own fennel juice using a juice extractor and a bulb of (Florence) fennel.

WHEATGRASS SALAD

4 sprigs fresh parsley
4 sprigs fresh cilantro
4 sprigs watercress
¹/₄ cucumber
2-inch round wheatgrass (see TIP)
still mineral water, well chilled, to taste

Wash and pat dry the cucumber, peel if pre-ferred, then coarsely chop and place in a blender. Wash and pat dry the herbs and watercress, and place in the blender. Set aside while preparing the wheatgrass.

Wash and pat dry the wheatgrass and then juice in a slow turning juicer. Add the juice to the cucumber and herbs. Blend for a few seconds until well blended, then serve at once, topped off with chilled mineral water, if preferred.

Serves 1

TIP: because wheatgrass deteriorates quickly, it should be juiced once everything else is prepared to ensure you are getting the freshest drink possible. You should be able to buy wheatgrass from a health food store and it comes still sprouting in cartons like mustard and cress. Snip the wheatgrass as close to the bottom as possible using scissors and measure it tightly bunched in "rounds" like spaghetti—a 2-inch round will yield about ¹/₄ cup of juice.

CUCUMBER & CARROT COMBO

1 medium cucumber
4 sprigs watercress
$^2/_3$ cup freshly pressed carrot juice or the yield from
   2 medium carrots
freshly ground black pepper to taste
few ice cubes, to serve

Wash and pat dry the cucumber. Halve and
scoop out the seeds using a teaspoon. Chop
coarsely and place in a blender.

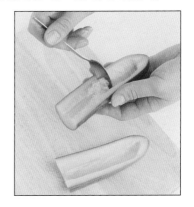

Wash and pat dry the watercress, trim if
necessary, and add to the cucmber.

Pour in the carrot juice and season lightly
with black pepper. Blend until smooth. Pour
over ice and sprinkle with extra pepper,
if liked.

Serves 2

VARIATION: wild arugula can be used
instead of the watercress.

MANGO & PEACH LASSI

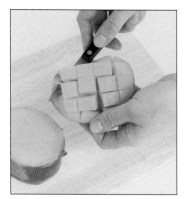

1 small or "mini" mango
1 ripe peach
1 lime
3/4 cup plain lowfat yogurt, well chilled
generous 1/3 cup water
1 teaspoon honey (optional)

To prepare the mango, rest it on its slimmest side and make 2 vertical cuts on either side of the flat central seed to remove the "cheeks." Score vertically and then horizontally across the flesh (1 inch apart) before turning the skin from underneath. Cut beneath each cube to remove from the skin.

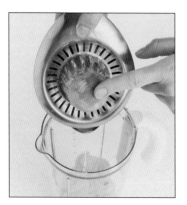

Peel away the skin from the fruit left around the seed and slice off the remaining flesh. Chop coarsely and place in a blender. Wash and pat dry the peach, cut in half, and remove the pit. Chop coarsely and place in the blender. Remove some lime zest for decoration and then extract the juice and pour into the blender along with the yogurt and water.

Blend for a few seconds, until smooth. Taste and sweeten with honey, if preferred. Pour into 2 glasses and serve sprinkled with the reserved lime zest.

Serves 2

VARIATION: if you prefer a thinner drink, then add a little lowfat milk.

— PEAR, MINT, & BLUEBERRY ICE —

juice of ½ lemon
1 ripe pear
8 medium fresh mint leaves, plus extra for garnish
⅝ cup frozen blueberries
¾ cup plain lowfat yogurt, well chilled
1 teaspoon honey

Extract the juice from the lemon and set aside. Working quickly, peel, core, and chop the pear, place in a blender and pour over the lemon juice.

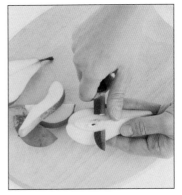

Wash and pat dry the mint leaves and place in the blender with the pear.

Add the frozen blueberries, yogurt, and honey and blend for a few seconds, until smooth. Pile into 2 glasses and decorate with a sprig of mint (if liked). Serve with a spoon.

Serves 2

VARIATION: this recipe is quite sweet but you can omit the honey for an even more healthful option.

PEACHY SOY BLEND

1 ripe peach
2 ripe apricots or 6 ready-to-eat dried apricots
$^{1}/_{2}$ small orange
$^{1}/_{2}$ cup peach-flavored soy yogurt
$^{1}/_{2}$ cup unsweetened soy milk, well chilled

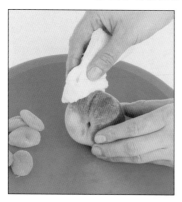

Wash and pat dry the peach and apricots (if fresh). Halve and remove the pits; chop coarsely and place in a blender, reserving 1 or 2 small slices for garnish (if liked).

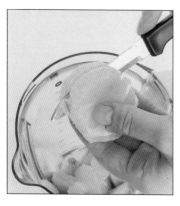

Peel and segment the orange, taking away as much of the white pith as possible. Chop the flesh and remove any seeds. Place in the blender.

Add the yogurt and pour in the milk. Blend for a few seconds, until smooth, and then pour into a tall glass. Thread the reserved peach on a toothpick (if liked) and serve with a straw.

Serves 1-2

VARIATION: for added flavor choose a variety of fruit-flavored soy yogurt. For extra nutrition, use calcium-enriched soy milk.

— DAIRY-FREE BANANA MILK —

1 large ripe banana
4 oz silken tofu, well chilled
½ cup unsweetened soy milk, well chilled
1 teaspoon thick honey
few drops vanilla extract, to taste

Peel the banana and slice thickly. Place in a blender.

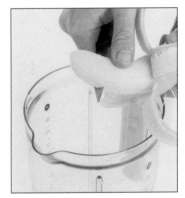

Drain the tofu, mash lightly with a fork, and add to the banana.

Pour in the milk, add the honey, and a few drops of vanilla extract. Blend for a few seconds, until thick and smooth. Pour into a large glass and serve with a straw.

Serves 1

TIP: silken tofu is very smooth and is the best for blending in drinks. It is available fresh or in vacuum cartons from the shelf. Firmer types will give a grainier texture when blended.

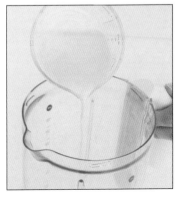

NUTTY PEAR

6 pecan halves
1 ripe pear
1 medium ripe banana
³/₄ cup rice milk, well chilled

Using the end of a rolling pin, lightly crush the pecans and place in a blender.

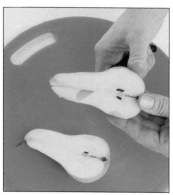

Working quickly, peel, core, and chop the pear, and peel and coarsely chop the banana. Place both in the blender.

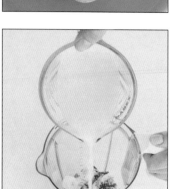

Pour in the rice milk and blend until smooth. Pour into a large glass to serve.

Serves 1

NOTE: rice milk is a light and refreshing alternative to dairy milk. It is made from brown rice and is cholesterol and lactose-free, low in fat, and has no added sugar.

BREAKFAST SMOOTHIE

6 pitted ready-to-eat prunes
6 dried ready-to-eat apricots
1 medium orange
pinch of ground cinnamon
1 tablespoon toasted oatmeal
1 cup oat milk, well chilled

Place the prunes and apricots in a small pan with 6 tablespoons water. Bring to a boil, cover, and let simmer gently for 10 minutes or until soft. Set aside to cool.

When ready to serve, peel the orange, removing as much of the white pith as possible. Chop coarsely and remove any seeds. Place in a blender along with the stewed prunes and apricots and any cooking liquid.

Add the cinnamon and oatmeal and then pour in the milk. Blend for a few seconds until smooth, and pour into a large glass.

Serves 1

TIP: soak and cook the fruit the night before so that you can enjoy this smoothie for breakfast the next day. Oat milk is soy, lactose, and cholesterol-free; it is suitable for vegetarians and has a well-balanced composition of protein, fat, and carbohydrates. It is filling and gentle on the stomach.

BRUNCH SHAKE

6 pitted dates
1 small cooking apple
1 medium ripe banana
$^1/_2$ cup plain soy yogurt, well chilled
$^1/_2$ cup unsweetened soy milk, well chilled
pinch of nutmeg
2 teaspoons wheat germ

Place the dates in a small pan. Peel, core, and chop the apple; add to the pan along with $^1/_2$ cup of water. Bring to a boil, cover, and let simmer gently for 10 minutes or until soft. Set aside to cool.

When ready to serve, peel and coarsely slice the banana, and place in a blender.

Add the date and apple mixture, yogurt, soy milk, and the nutmeg. Blend until thick and smooth. Divide among 2 glasses and serve each sprinkled with a teaspoon of wheat germ.

Serves 2

TIP: this very thick smoothie can be "watered down" with more soy milk, if preferred.

SWEET LASSI

2 cardamom pods
2/3 cup plain lowfat yogurt, well chilled
1/2 cup lowfat milk, well chilled
pinch of salt
1–2 teaspoons honey
pinch of finely grated lemon zest

Peel the green casing from the cardamom pods and remove the black seeds. Crush them finely using a mortar and pestle.

Mix the yogurt and milk with a pinch of salt and a little honey in a pitcher.

Stir in the lemon zest and all but a small pinch of the crushed seeds. Pour into a large glass and sprinkle over reserved cardamom.

Serves 1

NOTE: Lassis are drunk throughout India; they are cool and refreshing. Traditionally the drink is made with whole milk yogurt watered down with chilled water; this version is more healthful but just as delicious.

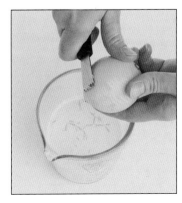

CHERRY BERRY

generous ³/₄ cup fresh sweet cherries
generous ³/₄ cup strawberries
¹/₂ cup cherry- or strawberry-flavored lowfat yogurt,
    well chilled
¹/₂ cup lowfat milk, well chilled
2 teaspoons maple syrup (optional)

Wash and pat dry the cherries and strawberries. Remove the pits from the cherries and place in a blender.

Hull the strawberries and add to the blender.

Add the yogurt and pour in the milk. Blend until thick and smooth. Taste and sweeten with the maple syrup, if using. Pour into 1 large glass, or 2 smaller ones, to serve.

Serves 1–2

— CARIBBEAN BANANA FREEZE —

1 large ripe banana
4 ice cubes
¾ cup buttermilk, well chilled
pinch of allspice, plus extra for dusting
2 teaspoons brown sugar

Peel the banana and chop coarsely. Place in a blender with the ice cubes.

Add the buttermilk to the banana and ice cubes.

Add a pinch of spice and the sugar. Blend until thick and smooth. Pile into a large glass and serve dusted with extra spice.

Serves 1

NOTE: buttermilk has a fresh, buttery taste; it is made from fat-free milk, cultured with a special bacteria to give it the distinctive taste, and with added milk solids to make it thick and creamy in texture.

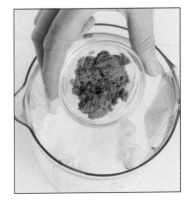

—— SPICED PLUM COOLER ——

2 cardamom pods
4 medium plums
pinch of ground cinnamon, plus extra for dusting
¹/₂ cup vanilla-flavored lowfat yogurt, well chilled
1 teaspoon thick honey
¹/₂ cup lowfat milk, well chilled

Peel the casing from the cardamom pods and remove the black seeds. Crush them finely using a mortar and pestle.

Wash and pat dry the plums, cut them in half, remove the pits, and cut into quarters. Place in the blender along with the crushed cardamom and a pinch of cinnamon.

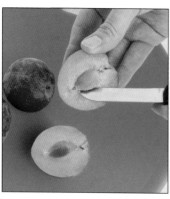

Spoon in the yogurt and honey and pour in the milk. Blend until creamy and smooth. Pour into a large glass, dust with extra cinnamon, and serve with a straw.

Serves 1

FRUITY BUTTERMILK

⅓ cup golden raisins
6 dried ready-to-eat apricots
½ cup freshly squeezed orange juice
½ cup apricot-flavored lowfat yogurt, well chilled
½ cup buttermilk, well chilled
pinch of finely grated orange zest, to serve

Place the golden raisins and apricots in a small pan and pour over the orange juice. Bring to a boil, cover, and let simmer gently for 10 minutes or until soft. Set aside to cool.

When ready to serve, transfer the raisin and apricot mixture to a blender along with any cooking juices.

Add the yogurt and buttermilk and then blend until thick and smooth. Pour into 1 large glass, or 2 smaller ones if sharing, and serve sprinkled with the orange zest.

Serves 1-2

CRANBERRY CRUSH

1 medium orange
1 $\frac{1}{8}$ cups frozen cranberries
1 cup vanilla-flavored lowfat yogurt, well chilled
1–2 teaspoons maple syrup

Peel the orange, removing as much of the white pith as possible. Chop the flesh and remove any seeds. Place in a blender.

Add the frozen cranberries to the blender.

Add the yogurt and a little maple syrup. Blend until creamy and smooth. Taste and add more maple syrup if necessary. Pile into 2 serving glasses and serve with a spoon.

Serves 2

JUST PEACHY PINEAPPLE

½ medium pineapple
2 ripe peaches
1 lime
4 oz silken tofu, well chilled
½ cup crushed ice

Peel and core the pineapple, chop the flesh coarsely, and place in a blender.

Wash and pat dry the peaches. Halve and remove the pits, chop coarsely, and then add to the pineapple and peaches.

Peel the lime, taking away as much of the white pith as possible. Chop the flesh and remove any seeds. Place in the blender along with the tofu. Blend until thick and smooth. Divide the crushed ice into 2 glasses and pour in the blended fruit.

Serves 2

TIP: a pineapple will smell "sweet" through its skin when it's ripe.

SPANISH TOMATO

6 medium ripe tomatoes on the vine
1 small red bell pepper
1 clove garlic
²/₃ cup plain lowfat dairy or soy yogurt, well chilled
2 teaspoons balsamic vinegar
pinch of smoked paprika
pinch of salt
few ice cubes, to serve
2 pitted green olives in brine, drained and chopped
  (optional)

Wash and pat dry the tomatoes and bell pepper. Remove the stems from the tomatoes and chop coarsely. Place in a blender.

Halve the bell pepper and remove the seeds. Chop and place in the blender. Peel the garlic and crush into the blender.

Spoon in the yogurt and vinegar, and add a pinch of paprika and salt. Blend until thick and smooth. Pour into 2 glasses over ice and serve sprinkled with the chopped olives, if liked.

Serves 2

HERBED GARLIC LASSI

4 sprigs fresh cilantro
4 sprigs fresh parsley, plus extra for garnish
6 whole fresh chives
1 clove garlic
pinch of salt and freshly ground black pepper
²/₃ cup plain lowfat yogurt, well chilled
¹/₂ cup lowfat milk, well chilled
few ice cubes, to serve

Wash and pat dry the herbs. Place in a blender.

Peel and crush the garlic into the blender. Season lightly.

Add the yogurt and pour in the milk. Blend until smooth. Pour over ice into a large glass and garnish with parsley to serve.

Serves 1

— DAIRY-FREE CARROT FRAPPE —

¹/₂ small lemon
1 small ripe avocado
²/₃ cup freshly pressed carrot juice or the yield from
    2 medium carrots
²/₃ cup plain soy yogurt, well chilled
¹/₂ cup crushed ice

Extract the juice from the lemon and set aside.

Halve the avocado, remove the pit and peel; chop coarsely and place in a blender with the lemon juice.

Pour in the carrot juice, add the yogurt, and crushed ice. Blend until thick and well crushed. Pour into a glass and serve.

Serves 1

SALSA VERDE

¼ cucumber
1 mild fresh green jalapeño chili
juice of 1 lime
6 sprigs cilantro
1 small ripe avocado
⅔ cup plain lowfat dairy or soy yogurt, well chilled
⅔ cup dairy or soy milk, well chilled

Wash and pat dry the cucumber and chili; chop the cucumber coarsely and place in a blender.

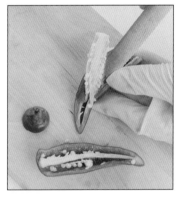

Halve and seed the chili; cut in half again and add to the blender. Extract the juice from the lime. Wash and shake dry the cilantro and add to the cucumber and chili.

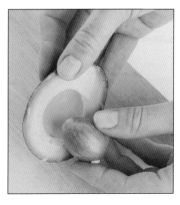

Halve the avocado, remove the pit and peel; chop coarsely and place in the blender with the lime juice. Add the yogurt and milk and blend, until creamy and smooth. Pile into a serving glass and serve with a spoon.

Serves 1-2

TIP: this is a thick smoothie so if you prefer something a little a thinner, add some fat-free milk to achieve your desired consistency.

TZATZIKI LASSI

$^1/_2$ cucumber
$^1/_2$ small red onion
12 medium fresh mint leaves, plus extra for garnish
1 cup plain lowfat dairy or soy yogurt, well chilled
pinch of salt

Wash and pat dry the cucumber. Slice off a few pieces for garnish, and coarsely chop the remainder. Place in a blender.

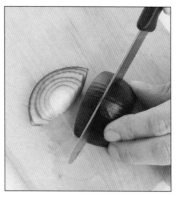

Peel the onion, chop coarsely, and add to the cucumber.

Wash and pat dry the mint leaves; add to the blender along with the yogurt and a little salt to season. Blend until smooth and pour over ice into 2 glasses. Serve with the reserved cucumber and garnish with some mint, if liked.

Serves 2

VARIATION: the raw onion adds "bite" to this drink but if preferred, replace with $^1/_2$ peeled and cored eating apple.

CARROT WITH A BITE

1 medium orange
²/₃ cup freshly pressed carrot juice or the yield from
    2 medium carrots
²/₃ cup plain lowfat dairy or soy yogurt, well chilled
few drops of Tabasco sauce, to taste
chili powder, for dusting

Peel the orange, taking away as much of the white pith as possible. Chop the flesh and remove any seeds. Place in a blender

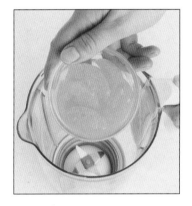

Pour in the carrot juice. Add the yogurt and a few drops of Tabasco sauce.

Blend until smooth and pour into a glass. Dust with chili powder to serve.

Serves 1

ENERGY BOOSTER PAPAYA

1 small papaya
1 ripe peach
2 passion fruit
$^2/_3$ cup freshly squeezed organic orange juice or the
  yield from 2 large oranges, juiced
1–2 acidophilus capsules (optional)

Peel the papaya, cut in half, and scoop out the seeds. Place the flesh in a blender.

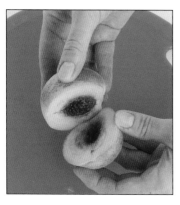

Wash and pat dry the peach, then halve, remove the pit, and add to the papaya. Halve the passion fruit and scoop the seeds into a small strainer. Strain the juice into the blender.

Pour in the orange juice. Open up the acidophilus capsules, if using, and stir into the smoothie. Blend for a few seconds until smooth. Pour into a large glass and serve at once.

Serves 1

TIP: always follow the manufacturer's recommended daily dosage for any supplement. This smoothie is best drunk on an empty stomach for the most benefit.

MEAL-IN-A-GLASS

1 small ripe avocado
4 tablespoons freshly squeezed lemon juice
6 whole fresh chives, plus extra for garnish
²/₃ cup freshly pressed carrot juice or the yield from
  2 medium carrots
²/₃ cup plain lowfat yogurt with live cultures, well
  chilled

Working quickly, halve the avocado and remove the pit, then peel and place in a blender with the lemon juice.

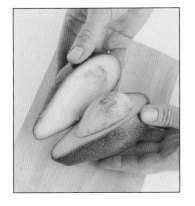

Wash and pat dry the chives. Using scissors, chop coarsely and add to the avocado.

Add the carrot juice and yogurt. Blend for a few seconds or until smooth. Pour into a glass and serve at once sprinkled with a few extra freshly chopped chives, if liked.

Serves 1

— "MORNING AFTER" DETOXER —

7 oz cooked peeled baby beet in natural juice
½-inch piece fresh ginger
2 tablespoons freshly squeezed lemon juice
⅔ cup freshly pressed carrot juice or the yield from
   2 medium carrots
⅔ cup freshly pressed apple juice or the yield from
   2 eating apples

Coarsely chop the beet and place in a blender with the juices from the package.

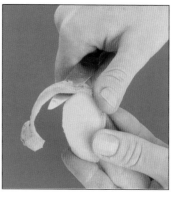

Peel and coarsely chop the ginger and add to the blender.

Pour in the remaining juices and blend until smooth. Pour into a glass and serve at once.

Serves 1

VARIATION: if you find the smoothie too concentrated, dilute it with some still mineral water. For a more powerful detoxer, juice 8 oz raw beet and a 2-inch piece fresh ginger and mix with the other juices.

— STRAWBERRY & CHAMOMILE —

1 chamomile tea bag
2-inch piece cinnamon stick
1 1/8 cups strawberries
1/2 cup freshly pressed apple juice or the yield from
   1 large eating apple, juiced
pinch ground cinnamon, for dusting (optional)

Place the tea bag and cinnamon stick in a small heatproof pitcher and pour over 1/2 cup boiling water. Leave to infuse for 5 minutes then discard the bag and cinnamon stick. Let cool.

When ready to serve, wash and pat dry the strawberries; remove the hulls, and place in a blender.

Pour in the apple juice and cold chamomile tea. Blend for a few seconds, until smooth; pour into a tall glass and serve dusted with ground cinnamon, if liked.

Serves 1

VARIATION: prepared chamomile tea bags are convenient and easy to use, but freshly dried flowers will give a stronger flavor.

ASIAN PICK-ME-UP

1 teaspoon good-quality Japanese green tea or 1
teabag
1 ripe kiwifruit
8 fresh litchis
500–1500 mg Korean ginseng extract (see TIP)
few ice cubes, to serve

Place the tea in a heatproof pitcher and
pour over scant 1 cup boiling water. Let
infuse for 3 minutes then strain to remove
the tea leaves, if using, or simply remove the
teabag. Let cool.

When ready to serve, peel and coarsely chop
the kiwifruit. Place in a blender. Peel the
litchis, cut in half, and remove the seeds.

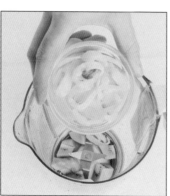

Add the litchis to the blender along with
the cold tea and ginseng. Blend until
smooth and pour over ice into a glass.

Serves 1

TIP: Korean ginseng extract is expensive
but believed to be of good quality. Always
read the manufacturer's daily dosage instructions—the powdered extract should come
with its own measuring spoon. Ginseng is
also available in ready-made capsule doses.

RASPBERRY IMMUNE BOOSTER

generous 1¾ cups raspberries, thawed if frozen,
  juices reserved
1 medium orange
1 teaspoon thick honey
approx. 1 ml alcohol-free extract of echinacea (see
  TIP)

Wash and pat dry the raspberries if using
fresh, and remove the hulls. Place in a
blender. If the fruit has been frozen, add the
juices as well.

Peel and segment the orange, removing as
much of the white pith as possible. Chop
coarsely, discarding any seeds, and place in
the blender. Add the honey and echinacea.
Blend until smooth, pour into a glass, and
serve at once.

Serves 1-2

TIP: for maximum benefit, drink on an
empty stomach. The quantity of echinacea
you add to your smoothie will depend on
how diluted the product is to start with, so
always refer to the manufacturer's daily
dosage instructions. If you find this
smoothie too thick, dilute it with a little
still mineral water.

MEGA VITAMIN C TONIC

1 large orange
1 lemon
1 lime
¹/₂ pink grapefruit
1 teaspoon honey

Peel all of the citrus fruit, removing as much of the white pith as possible.

Chop the fruit coarsely, discarding any seeds, and place in a blender.

Add the honey and blend for a few seconds until smooth. Pour over crushed ice to serve.

Serves 1

VARIATION: for a refreshing, longer, less-concentrated drink, divide this smoothie between 2 glasses and top off with sparkling mineral water.

BUSY BEE'S COMFORTER

1 lemon, plus the freshly squeezed juice of another
  lemon
²/₃ cup plain whole dairy or soy milk, at room
  temperature
1–2 teaspoon thick honey
approx. 2 teaspoons bee pollen grains (see
  ALLERGY WARNING and NOTE)

Peel the whole lemon, slicing off as much of
the white pith as possible. Chop coarsely,
discarding any seeds, and place in a blender
along with the lemon juice.

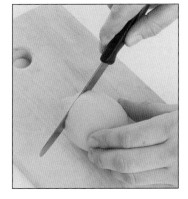

Spoon in the yogurt and blend until
smooth. Taste and sweeten with the honey,
as necessary. Stir in the bee pollen and
transfer to a glass and serve.

Serves 1

ALLERGY WARNING: not suitable for
those with an allergy to pollen, i.e. hay fever
sufferers.

NOTE: bee pollen is also available in
capsule form. The quantity you add to your
smoothie will depend on how diluted the
product is to start with, so always refer to
the manufacturer's daily dosage instructions.

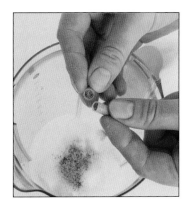

—— DAIRY-FREE NUTTY MILK ——

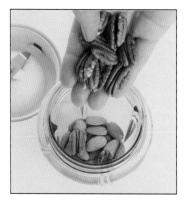

$^1/_8$ cup whole shelled almonds
$^1/_4$ cup shelled pecan halves
1 tablespoon pepitas
1 $^1/_4$ cups still mineral water
$^1/_2$ teaspoon ground cinnamon, plus extra for dusting
few ice cubes, to serve (optional)
1 teaspoon honey

When ready to serve, grind the nuts and seeds together in a spice grinder or small food processor—the mixture must be very fine in order to obtain a good blend.

Transfer to a small pitcher and gradually blend in the water. Mix in the cinnamon and honey.

Pour into a glass, over ice if liked, and dust with the cinnamon.

Serves 1-2

TIP: this drink is an excellent source of protein and is delicious served over ice. Store opened packages of nuts and seeds well sealed in the refrigerator in order to keep them as fresh as possible.

BERRY BOOSTER

1 1/8 cups blueberries, thawed if frozen, juices
   reserved
1/2 cup cranberries, thawed if frozen, juices reserved
1/2 cup freshly pressed orange juice or the yield from
   2 medium oranges, juiced
1 tablespoon wheat germ
1–2 teaspoons thick honey

Wash and pat dry the blueberries and cranberries, if using fresh.

Place the berries in a blender. If the fruit has
been frozen, add the juices as well.

Pour in the orange juice and 2 teaspoons
wheat germ. Blend until smooth. Taste and
add honey to sweeten as necessary. Pour
into a glass and serve sprinkled with the
remaining wheat germ.

Serves 1

TIP: blueberries contain a substance, which
helps enable the intestinal tract to stay
clean and healthy and, like cranberries, are
rich in antioxidants.

FULL OF FIBER

1³/₈ cups raspberries, thawed if frozen, juices reserved
¹/₃ cup freshly squeezed orange juice or the yield from 1 large orange, juiced
¹/₃ cup oat milk, well chilled
¹/₃ cup plain lowfat dairy or soy yogurt with live cultures, well chilled
1¹/₂ oz fine oatmeal
2 teaspoons wheat bran
1 teaspoon honey (optional)

Wash and pat dry the raspberries if using fresh, and remove the hulls. Place in a blender. If the fruit has been frozen, add the juices as well. Pour in the orange juice.

Add the oatmeal and 1 teaspoon wheat bran. Then add the oat milk and spoon in the yogurt. Blend until smooth. Taste and sweeten, if necessary. Pour into a glass, sprinkle with remaining wheat bran, and serve with a spoon.

Serves 1

– CARING, SHARING SMOOTHIE –

6 shelled Brazil nuts
1 lemon
1 medium ripe banana
1 small ripe avocado
1 teaspoon honey
1¹/₄ cups plain lowfat dairy or soy milk, well chilled
2 teaspoons wheat germ

When ready to serve, grind the nuts in a spice grinder or small food processor—the mixture must be very fine in order to obtain a good blend.

Peel the lemon, slicing off as much of the white pith as possible. Working quickly, chop coarsely, discarding any seeds. Peel and coarsely chop the banana.

Halve the avocado and remove the pit. Peel and coarsely chop. Place the nuts, lemon, banana, and avocado in a blender along with the honey and milk. Blend until smooth. Pour into 2 serving glasses and sprinkle each portion with wheat germ.

Serves 2

TIP: this is a lusciously thick and decadent protein-rich drink, ideal for sharing—add more milk, if preferred.

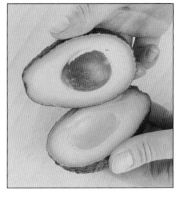

FLAXEN PEAR

1 ripe pear
1 tablespoon flax seed
¹/₂ cup plain lowfat dairy or soy milk, well chilled
¹/₂ cup plain lowfat dairy or soy yogurt, well chilled
1 teaspoon honey, plus extra for decoration
   (optional)

Working quickly, peel, core, and chop the pear and place in a blender.

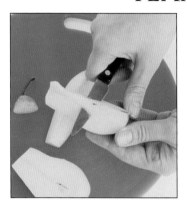

Grind the seeds in a spice grinder or small food processor—the mixture must be very fine in order to obtain a good blend.

Add the ground seeds to the blender. Pour in the milk and add the yogurt. Blend until smooth and add honey to taste. Pour into a glass, drizzle over some honey (if liked), and serve at once.

Serves 1

TIP: if you prefer, replace the whole seeds with 1 tablespoon flax seed oil.

—— AVOCADO CHARGER ——

1 scallion
1 clove garlic
1 small ripe avocado
2 oz alfalfa sprouts, plus extra for garnish
4 oz silken tofu
½ cup mineral water, plus extra to taste, well chilled

Trim and coarsely chop the scallion.

Peel and crush the garlic. Place in a blender with the scallion.

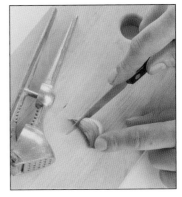

Working quickly, halve the avocado and remove the pit. Peel and coarsely chop and place in the blender. Add the sprouts, tofu, and water and blend until thick, creamy, and smooth. Stir in enough water until you obtain the texture you require. Serve sprinkled with alfalfa sprouts, if liked.

Serves 1

TIP: alfalfa sprouts are one of the most nutritionally valuable plants we can eat so this smoothie is highly nutritious.

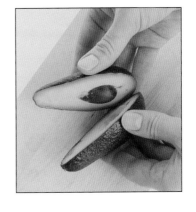

— BANANA VITALITY SHAKE —

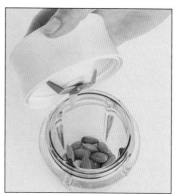

¹/₈ cup whole shelled almonds
1 large ripe banana
²/₃ cup lowfat milk
²/₃ cup plain lowfat yogurt with live cultures
1 small organic egg (see WARNING), or 1
   tablespoon protein powder (or as directed)
2 teaspoons wheat germ
1–2 teaspoons maple syrup to taste
pinch of freshly grated nutmeg

Grind the almonds in a spice grinder or small food processor—the mixture must be very fine in order to obtain a good blend.

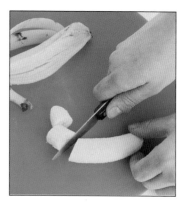

Peel and coarsely chop the banana and place in a blender along with the ground almonds. Add the milk, yogurt, egg (or protein powder if using), and wheat germ to the blender and blend for a few seconds until smooth. Add maple syrup to taste, then pour into a glass and serve at once sprinkled with nutmeg.

Serves 1

WARNING: raw egg should not be eaten by the elderly, children, babies, pregnant women, or those with an impaired immune system because there can be a risk of contracting salmonella. If you prefer, you can add protein powder as directed instead of the egg—see manufacturer's directions for quantities.

— STRAWBERRY SORBET FLOAT —

1 ⅛ cups strawberries
1 ice cream scoop of strawberry sherbet
few drops good-quality vanilla extract
⅔ cup pink lemonade, well chilled
6 white mini marshmallows

Wash and pat dry the strawberries.

Halve and remove the hulls, then place in a blender.

Add the sherbet and vanilla and blend until smooth. Transfer to a glass and carefully pour in the lemonade, stirring until well blended. Serve at once, topped with the marshmallows, while frothy and fizzing.

Serves 1-2

RASPBERRY RIPPLE

1³/₈ cups raspberries, thawed if frozen, juices reserved
¹/₂ cup whole milk, well chilled
¹/₂ cup plain whole milk yogurt, well chilled
1 ice cream scoop raspberry-flavored yogurt ice
2 teaspoons raspberry syrup or sauce

Wash and pat dry the raspberries, if using fresh. Remove the hulls and place in a blender. If the fruit has been frozen, add the juices as well.

Pour in the milk and add the yogurt. Blend until thick and creamy.

Pile into a glass and top with a scoop of yogurt ice. Drizzle with the syrup or sauce and serve at once with a straw and a long-handled spoon.

Serves 1

TIP: for a lower fat version use lowfat milk and yogurt.

CANDY APPLETASTIC

1 eating apple
$^1/_2$ cup freshly pressed apple juice or the yield from
   1 large eating apple, juiced
$^2/_3$ cup lowfat milk, well chilled
1 tablespoon lowfat milk powder
2 teaspoons toffee or caramel syrup or sauce
few ice cubes, to serve

Peel, core, and coarsely chop the eating apple.

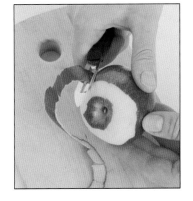

Place in a blender together with the apple juice.

Pour in the milk and then add the milk powder. Blend until thick and smooth. Pour into a glass over ice (if liked), and drizzle in the syrup.

Serves 1-2

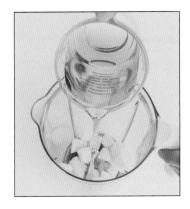

— BUTTERY BANANA FREEZE —

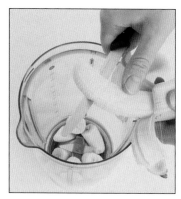

1 large ripe banana
¹/₂ cup lowfat milk
2 ice cream scoops butterscotch-flavored ice cream
4 ice cubes
2 teaspoons butterscotch, crushed

Working quickly, peel and coarsely chop the banana and place in a blender.

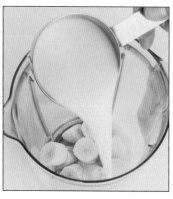

Pour in the milk; add one scoop of ice cream and the ice cubes. Blend until smooth and thick.

Pile into a glass and top with the remaining scoop of ice cream and a sprinkling of crushed butterscotch. Serve at once with a long-handled spoon.

Serves 1

VARIATION: for an icier version, freeze the banana pieces for about 30 minutes or until firm, and blend them as above.

PEACH NECTAR

1 rose hip tea bag
1 ripe peach
³/₄ cup strained plain yogurt, well chilled
1 teaspoon thick Greek honey
pinch of ground cinnamon, plus extra to serve
few drops of rose water extract, to taste

Place the tea bag in a heatproof pitcher and pour over ²/₃ cup boiling water. Leave to infuse for 5 minutes then strain to remove the tea bag. Set aside to cool.

When ready to serve, wash and pat dry the peach; halve and remove the pit. Coarsely chop and place in a blender.

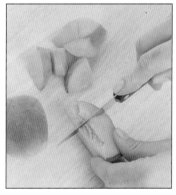

Add the yogurt and remaining ingredients, and pour in the cold tea. Blend until thick and creamy. Pour into a glass and serve at once, sprinkled with cinnamon, if liked.

Serves 1

NEAPOLITAN

¹/₂ cup strawberries
¹/₂ medium banana
2 ice cream scoops good-quality chocolate flavored
   ice cream
2 ice cream scoops good-quality vanilla flavored
   ice cream
few drops good-quality vanilla extract, to taste
¹/₄ cup lowfat milk, well chilled
1 teaspoon lowfat milk powder
1 teaspoon grated semisweet chocolate

Wash and pat dry the strawberries and remove the hulls. Blend until smooth and thick. Transfer to a glass and set aside.

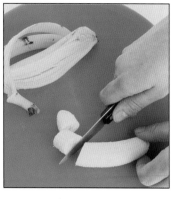

Peel and coarsely chop the banana and place in a clean blender. Working quickly, add the chocolate ice cream and blend until smooth and thick. Carefully spoon over the strawberry puree.

In a clean blender, blend the vanilla ice cream with a few drops vanilla extract, the milk and milk powder, and then carefully spoon on top of the chocolate layer. Sprinkle with the grated chocolate and serve immediately.

Serves 1

KNICKERBOCKER FLOAT

1 ripe peach
generous ⅝ cup raspberries, thawed if frozen,
  juices reserved
1 kiwifruit
¾ cup plain whole dairy milk or soy yogurt
2 teaspoons fruit syrup or sauce

Wash and pat dry the peach. Halve and remove the pit, coarsely chop, and set aside.

Peel and coarsely chop the kiwifruit. Wash and pat dry the raspberries, if fresh, and remove the hulls.

Blend each of the fruit separately with ¼ cup yogurt, and layer up in a serving glass. Spoon over the syrup or sauce and serve at once with a long-handled spoon.

Serves 1

VARIATION: for a more healthful version, use plain lowfat yogurt.

CARIBBEAN DREAM

¹/₄ medium ripe pineapple
1 medium ripe banana
1 tablespoon cream of coconut
²/₃ cup plain lowfat dairy or soy milk, well chilled
pinch of freshly grated nutmeg
1–2 teaspoons maple syrup (optional)
1 teaspoon toasted coconut shavings

Slice the pineapple, remove the core, and peel. Chop coarsely and place in a blender.

Peel and coarsely chop the banana and add to the pineapple. Spoon in the coconut, add the milk, and a pinch of nutmeg.

Blend for a few seconds until thick, creamy, and smooth. Taste and sweeten with maple syrup, if liked. Pour into a large glass and serve sprinkled with the toasted coconut.

Serves 1

TIP: cream of coconut is a thick, concentrated form of coconut compound and is usually available in cartons. If desired, replace with light coconut milk for a more healthful version.

BLUEBERRY NEW YORKER

generous ³/₄ cup blueberries, thawed if frozen, juices
  reserved
¹/₄ cup reduced-fat cream cheese, well chilled
1 tablespoon maple syrup
few drops of good-quality vanilla extract
¹/₂ cup lowfat milk, well chilled

Wash and pat dry the blueberries if using
fresh. Place in a blender. If the fruit has
been frozen, add the juices as well.

Spoon in the cream cheese and maple syrup
and add a few drops of vanilla.

Pour in the milk and blend until thick and
smooth. Transfer to a serving glass and serve
with shortbread, if desired.

Serves 1

TIP: if you want to be even more indulgent,
replace the reduced-fat cheese and milk
with whole fat options.

KEY LIME FREEZE

2 limes
2 ice cream scoops of lime or lemon sherbet
$\frac{1}{2}$ cup sweetened condensed milk
$\frac{1}{2}$ cup light cream, well chilled

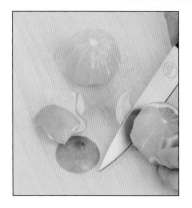

Slice off a few thin strips of lime and shred; set aside. Peel the limes, slicing off as much of the white pith as possible. Chop coarsely, discarding any seeds, and place in a blender.

Add the sherbet and spoon in the condensed milk.

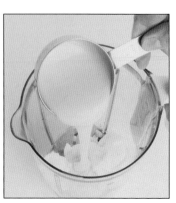

Pour in the cream and blend until smooth. Pile into 2 serving glasses and serve at once, sprinkled with the reserved shredded lime.

Serves 2

— DOUBLE CHOCOLATE VELVET —

2 tablespoons chocolate syrup
1 cup chocolate-flavored lowfat milk, well chilled
$1/3$ cup light cream, well chilled
2 scoops good-quality chocolate-flavored ice cream
2 tablespoons dark chocolate sauce
1 milk chocolate flake, crushed or $1\frac{1}{2}$ oz flaked milk chocolate
few ice cubes, to serve

Spoon the chocolate syrup (reserving a little for decoration) into a blender.

Pour in the chocolate milk and cream, and add the ice cream. Blend until smooth and well mixed.

Divide between 2 tall glasses and swirl in the chocolate sauce and half the chocolate flake using a cocktail stirrer. Top off with the ice cubes (if liked) and serve at once sprinkled with the remaining chocolate flake and drizzled with the reserved syrup.

Serves 2

—— STRAWBERRY DELIGHT ——

1 1/8 cups strawberries
2 scoops white chocolate-flavored ice cream
1/4 cup ricotta cheese
1/2 cup whole milk, well chilled
2 tablespoons crushed graham crackers
2 teaspoons strawberry sauce

Wash and pat dry the strawberries, and remove the hulls. Slice in half and place in a blender.

Add the white chocolate ice cream to the strawberries.

Add the ricotta cheese, and milk and blend until thick and smooth. Pile into 2 serving glasses and drizzle over the sauce. Serve at once topped with the crushed crackers.

Serves 2

CHOCORANGE

⅛ cup heavy or whipping cream
1 tablespoon chocolate syrup
1 medium orange
1 ice cream scoop orange-flavored sherbet
⅔ cup chocolate-flavored lowfat milk, well chilled
unsweetened cocoa powder, for dusting

Spoon the cream into a bowl and whip until it forms soft peaks. Reserve 1 tablespoon and set aside. Carefully fold the chocolate syrup into the remaining cream. Cover and chill until required.

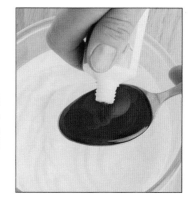

Peel the orange, removing as much of the white pith as possible. Chop coarsely, discarding any seeds, and place in a blender. When ready to serve, add the sherbet to the blender.

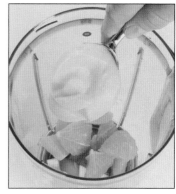

Add the chocolate milk and blend until thick and smooth. Pour into a serving glass and top with the reserved whipped cream. Serve at once, dusted with cocoa powder.

Serves 1

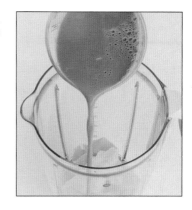

ICED CAFE AU LAIT

1–2 tablespoons liquid coffee extract
2 cups vanilla nonfat frozen yogurt
6 ice cubes
¹/₂ cup lowfat milk, well chilled
2 teaspoons grated bittersweet chocolate
2 chocolate-coated coffee beans, to serve (optional)

Depending on how strong you like your coffee, spoon the coffee extract into a blender.

Then, working quickly, add the frozen yogurt to the coffee.

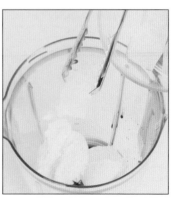

Add the ice cubes and pour in the milk. Blend until finely crushed and smooth. Pile into 2 serving cups or glasses and sprinkle with bittersweet chocolate. Serve at once, topped with a chocolate-coated coffee bean (if liked), with spoons.

Serves 2

— PEANUT BUTTER & COOKIES —

2 medium ripe bananas
1/2 cup lowfat milk, well chilled
2 tablespoons smooth peanut butter
2 scoops vanilla nonfat frozen yogurt
6 chocolate cream cookies, finely crushed

Working quickly, peel and coarsely chop the bananas. Place in a blender.

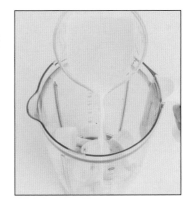

Pour in the milk, then spoon in the peanut butter and frozen yogurt. Blend until thick and smooth. Fold in all but 1 tablespoon of the crushed cookies.

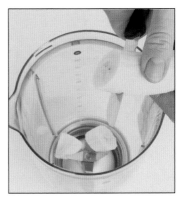

Divide between 2 serving glasses and serve at once, sprinkled with the remaining crushed cookie, with spoons.

Serves 2

TIP: to crush the cookies easily, place in a clean plastic bag, seal, and crush finely with a rolling pin.

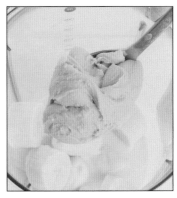

—— "IN THE PINK" SORBET ——

1 pink grapefruit
1 lemon
1 tablespoon grenadine syrup
2 ice cream scoops lemon sherbet
1 cup crushed ice

Peel the grapefruit (reserving a little for garnish) and lemon, slicing off as much of the white pith as possible. Chop coarsely, discarding any seeds, and place in a blender.

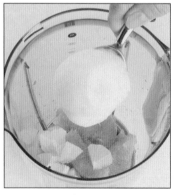

Add the syrup, sherbet, and crushed ice, and blend until smooth and thick.

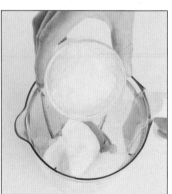

Transfer to 2 serving glasses, garnish with the reserved grapefruit (if liked) and serve immediately.

Serves 2

RASPBERRY RAZZLE

2 medium oranges
1 3/8 cups raspberries, thawed if frozen, juices
  reserved
4 ice cubes
3/4 cup sparkling elderberry flower drink, well chilled

Peel the oranges, removing as much of the white pith as possible. Chop coarsely, discarding any seeds, and place in a blender.

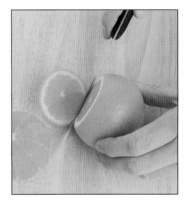

Wash and pat dry the raspberries, if fresh, and remove stems and hulls, if necessary. Place in the blender and if the fruit has been frozen, add the juices.

Add the ice cubes. Blend until smooth. Pour into 2 serving glasses. Top off with sparkling elderberry flower drink and serve at once with a stirrer.

Serves 2

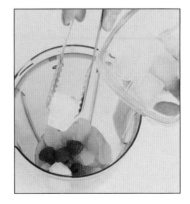

– ANGELIC TROPICAL DAIQUIRI –

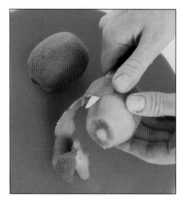
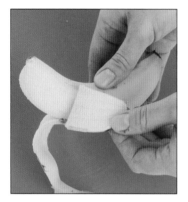

1 ripe banana
2 kiwifruit
juice of 1 lime
1/2 cup freshly pressed apple juice or the yield from
   1 large eating apple
1 teaspoon banana syrup
2 cups crushed ice

Working quickly, peel and coarsely chop the banana and place in a blender.

Peel the kiwifruit and chop coarsely. Add to the banana.

Add the lime and apple juices, banana syrup, and ice, and blend until smooth and slushy. Pile into 2 large cocktail glasses or champagne flutes and serve at once.

Serves 2

GINGER MELON FIZZ

½ orange melon, such as cantaloupe or Charantais
2 small lemons
2 pieces preserved ginger in syrup
few ice cubes, to serve
1 cup dry ginger ale, well chilled

Scoop out the melon seeds. Cut into slices, remove the skin, and chop coarsely. Place in a blender.

Peel the lemons, slicing off as much of the white pith as possible. Chop coarsely, discarding any seeds, and add to the blender.

Chop the ginger and place in the blender. Blend for a few seconds until smooth. Divide between 2 serving glasses and add a few ice cubes to each. Top off with dry ginger and serve with a stirrer.

Serves 2

TIP: for a sweeter version, use alcohol-free ginger beer.

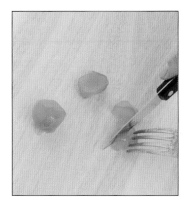

TROPICAL TEASER

1/4 medium ripe pineapple
1/2 lime
2 oz fresh coconut meat
3/4 cup light coconut milk
2 cups crushed ice
2 tablespoons grenadine syrup

Peel and core the pineapple, chop coarsely, and place in a blender.

Extract the juice from the lime and add to the pineapple.

Coarsely chop the coconut and add to the blender. Pour in the coconut milk and blend until smooth and thick. Transfer to a cocktail shaker, add the ice and syrup, and shake for a few seconds to blend and chill. Pour into 2 glasses and serve at once.

Serves 2

PEACHES & CREAM

2 ripe peaches
¹/₂ cup reduced-fat cream
2 ice cream scoops peach-flavored sherbet
1 cup crushed ice
2 teaspoons raspberry syrup, to serve (optional)

Wash and pat dry the peaches. Cut in half and remove the pits. Chop coarsely and place in a blender.

Pour in the cream and then add the peach sherbet.

Add the crushed ice and blend for a few seconds, until smooth and crushed. Pile into 2 serving glasses, drizzle with raspberry syrup (if desired), and serve with spoons.

Serves 2

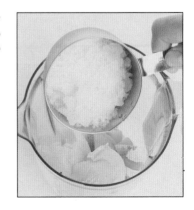

PINEAPPLE PASSION

¹/₂ medium papaya
2 ripe guavas
1 Golden passion fruit
1 cup freshly pressed pineapple juice or the yield
   from 1 lb 4 oz fresh pineapple
2 tablespoons maracuja (passion fruit) syrup
2 cups crushed ice

Peel the papaya and scoop out the black seeds. Coarsely chop the flesh (reserving a little for garnish) and place in a blender. Peel the guavas and discard the seeds if necessary (see TIP). Place in the blender.

Cut the passion fruit in half and scoop out the seeds into the blender.

Pour in the pineapple juice and blend until smooth. Pile into a cocktail shaker and add the syrup and crushed ice. Shake to mix and let chill. Divide between 2 large cocktail glasses, garnish with the reserved papaya (if liked) and serve at once.

Serves 2

TIP: guava seeds are sometimes soft enough to eat, but in large fruits they are often hard and should be discarded.

MIXED BERRY SHERBET

generous ³/₄ cup strawberries
³/₈ cup raspberries, thawed if frozen, juices reserved
³/₈ cup blackberries, thawed if frozen, juices reserved
³/₈ cup blueberries, thawed if frozen, juices reserved
2 tablespoons strawberry syrup
1 egg white (see WARNING)
6 ice cubes

Wash and pat dry the fruits, if using fresh. Hull the berries if necessary, and place in a blender. If the fruit has been frozen, add the juices as well.

Add the syrup and blend for a few seconds, until smooth. In a bowl, whisk the egg white until thick and foaming, but not stiff. Transfer to the blender along with the ice cubes. Blend for a few seconds, until slushy and foaming. Pour into 2 glasses and serve at once.

Serves 2

WARNING: raw egg should not be eaten by the elderly, children, babies, pregnant women, or those with an impaired immune system because there can be a risk of contracting salmonella. You can leave the egg white out of this recipe but the result will be icier.

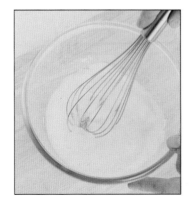

CRANCHEE CRUSH

12 fresh litchis
1¹/₈ cups frozen cranberries
2 tablespoons grenadine syrup
low-calorie tonic water, well chilled, to taste
few mint leaves, to garnish (optional)

Peel the litchis and remove the seeds. Place in a blender.

Add the frozen cranberries to the litchis.

Add the syrup and blend until smooth and crushed. Divide the mixture between 2 chilled serving glasses and top off with tonic water to taste. Serve at once garnished with the mint leaves, if liked.

Serves 2

VARIATION: for a sweeter version, use lemonade instead of tonic water.

ICED PEAR & PINEAPPLE

½ lemon
4 slices ripe fresh pineapple
2 ripe pears
1 tablespoon almond syrup or a few drops pure
  almond extract
8 ice cubes

Extract the juice from the lemon and set aside.

Remove the skin from the pineapple. Coarsely chop, removing the core.

Peel and core the pears. Coarsely chop and place in the blender along with the lemon juice, pineapple, almond syrup or extract, and the ice cubes. Blend until smooth and well crushed. Pile into 2 glasses and serve at once with spoons.

Serves 2

TIP: for a longer drink, top off with well-chilled sparkling mineral water.

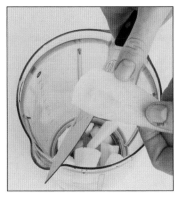

BLACK VELVET FIZZ

1½ cups black currants, thawed if frozen, juice
   reserved
⅔ cup freshly pressed apple juice or the yield from
   2 eating apples, juiced
2 tablespoons black currant syrup (syrop de cassis)
   or black currant cordial
few ice cubes, to serve
sparkling mineral water, well chilled, to taste

If using fresh black currants, wash and pat
dry and pull the currants from the stems;
place in a blender. If the fruit has been
frozen, add the juices as well.

Pour in the apple juice and add the black
currant syrup or cordial. Blend until smooth
and well blended.

Pour into 2 glasses and add a few ice cubes
to each. Top off with sparkling mineral
water to taste. Serve at once.

Serves 2

—— MANGO COLADA FRAPPE ——

1 medium ripe mango
2 oz fresh coconut meat
³/₄ cup light coconut milk
¹/₂ cup freshly pressed pineapple juice or the yield
   from 14 oz fresh pineapple, juiced
8 ice cubes

To prepare the mango, rest it on its slimmest side and make 2 vertical cuts on either side of the flat central seed to remove the "cheeks." Score vertically and then horizontally across the flesh (1 inch apart) before turning the skin from underneath. Slice each cube from the skin.

Peel away the skin from the fruit left around the seed and slice off the remaining flesh. Chop coarsely and place in a blender. Coarsely chop the fresh coconut and add to the blender.

Pour in the coconut milk, pineapple juice, and add the ice cubes. Blend until smooth, crushed, and thick. Transfer to 2 glasses and serve immediately with spoons.

Serves 2

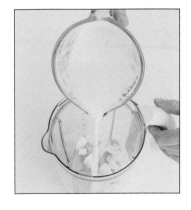

INDEX